PIANO · VOCAL · GUITAR

ALICIA KEYS

AS I AM

ISBN 978-1-4234-3584-6

HAL•LEONARD®
CORPORATION
7777 W. BLUEMOUND RD. P.O. BOX 13819 MILWAUKEE, WI 53213

In Australia Contact:
Hal Leonard Australia Pty. Ltd.
4 Lentara Court
Cheltenham, Victoria, 3192 Australia
Email: ausadmin@halleonard.com.au

Visit Hal Leonard Online at
www.halleonard.com

CONTENTS

AS I AM
(Intro)

Words and Music by
ALICIA KEYS

Slowly, very expressively

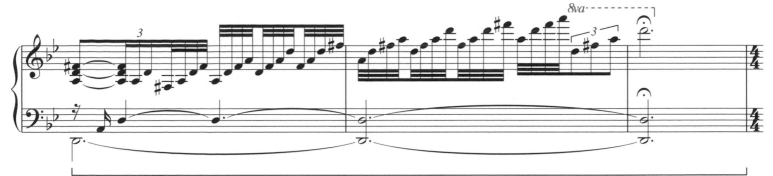

Moderately, steadily

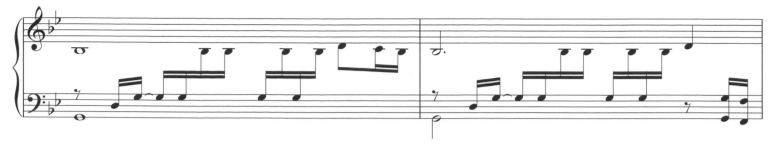

GO AHEAD

Words and Music by ALICIA KEYS, KERRY BROTHERS, JR.,
MARK BATSON and MARSHA AMBROSIUS

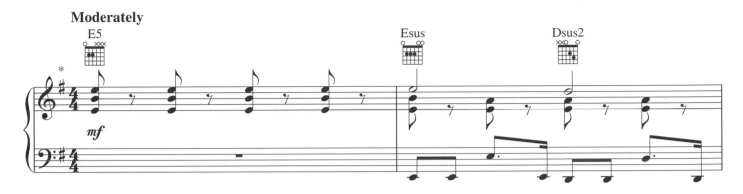

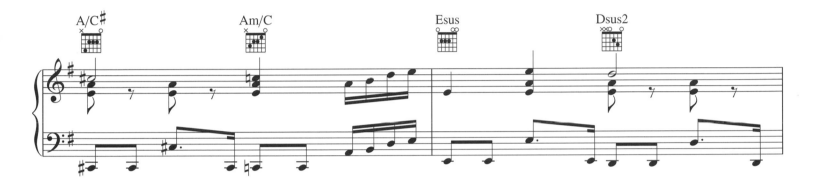

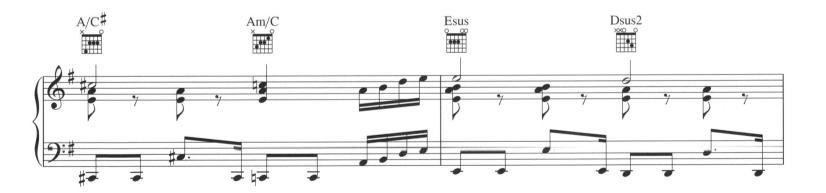

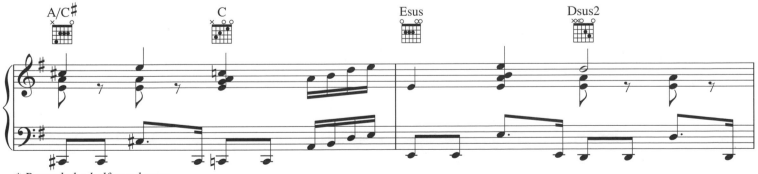

Recorded a half step lower.

boy, you've dis - ap - point - ed me.
so you best be on your way.
(I thought you gave me love;

was nev - er near e - nough. Soon e - nough, time re - vealed

no way to what is real. No one - 'll need to know.

Boy, see, you got - ta go. What have you giv - en me but

madeup my mind this time, and I'm donewith you. Noth - ing you can say or can do can

make me change my mind. So just...

D.S. al Coda

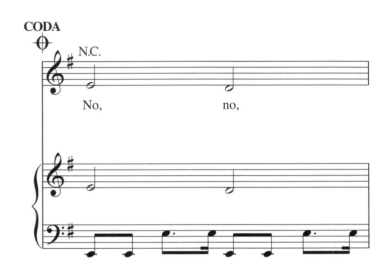

CODA

N.C.

No,   no,

no,   no.   No,   no,

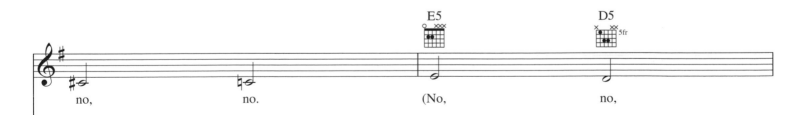

no,   no.   (No,   no,

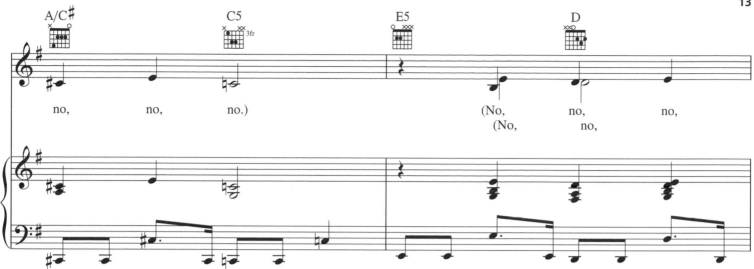

no,   no,   no.)   (No,   no,   no,
(No,   no,

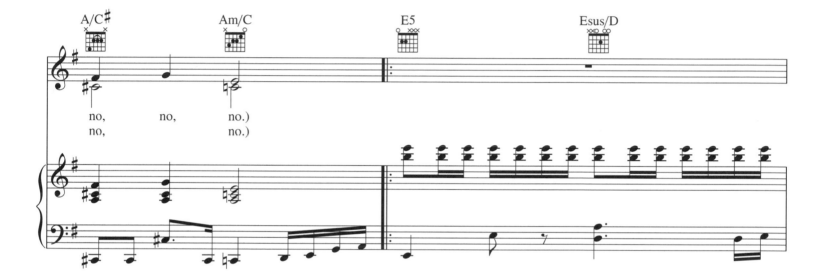

no,   no,   no.)
no,   no.)

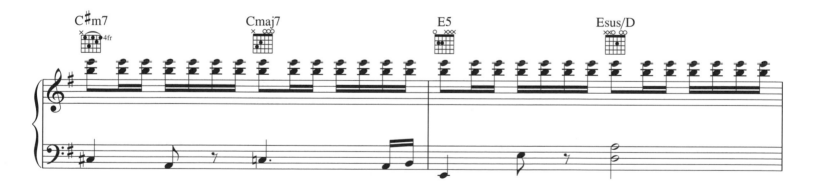

Optional Ending

Repeat and fade

SUPERWOMAN

Words and Music by ALICIA KEYS,
LINDA PERRY and STEVE MOSTYN

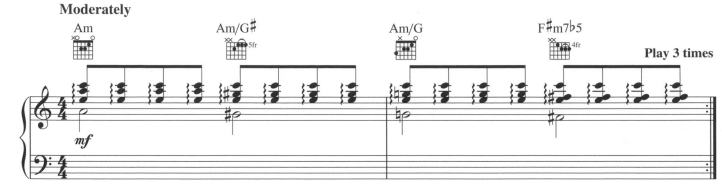

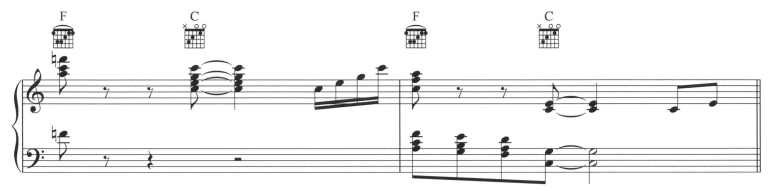

Ev - 'ry - where _ I'm turn - ing, ___

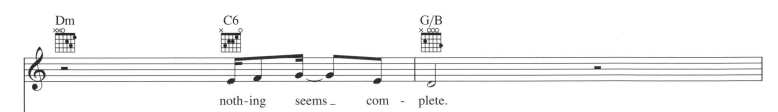

noth - ing seems _ com - plete.

I stand — up and — I'm search - ing —

for the bet - ter part of me. —

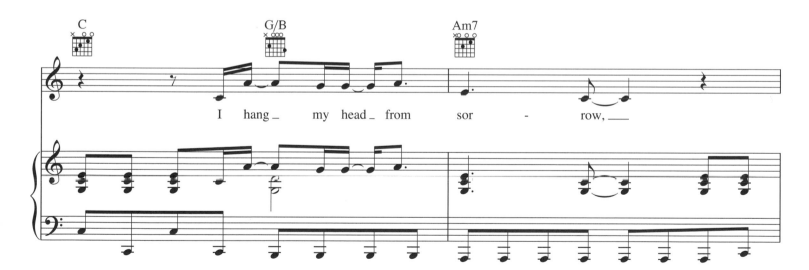

I hang — my head — from sor - row, —

slave to hu - man - i - ty. —

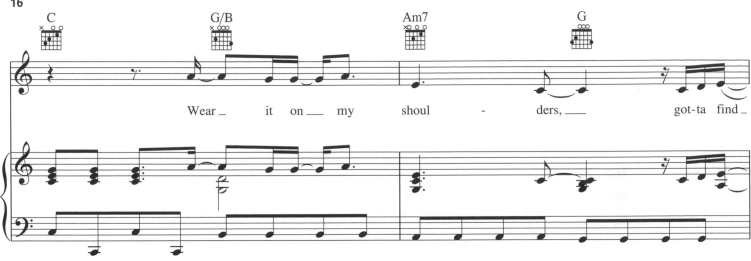

Wear _ it on _ my shoul - ders, _ got-ta find _

the strength _ in me. _ 'Cause

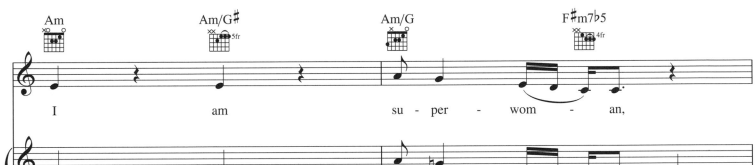

I am su - per - wom - an,

yes, I am _ (yes, she is). _

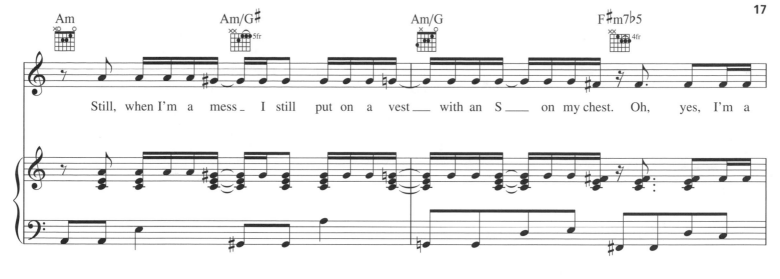

Still, when I'm a mess__ I still put on a vest__ with an S__ on my chest. Oh, yes, I'm a

su - per - wom - an._____ This is for,

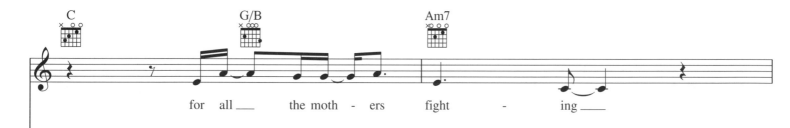

for all __ the moth - ers fight - ing __

for bet - ter days to come,_____

and all my wom-en, all my wom-en sit-tin' here try - in'

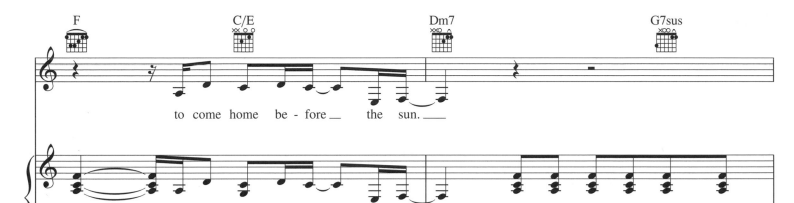

to come home be - fore the sun.

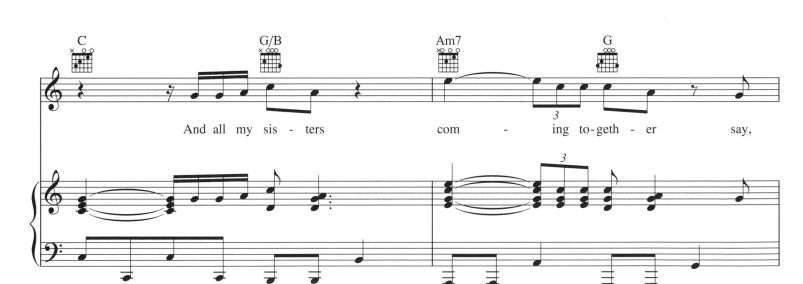

And all my sis - ters com - ing to-geth - er say,

"Yes I will, yes I can." 'Cause

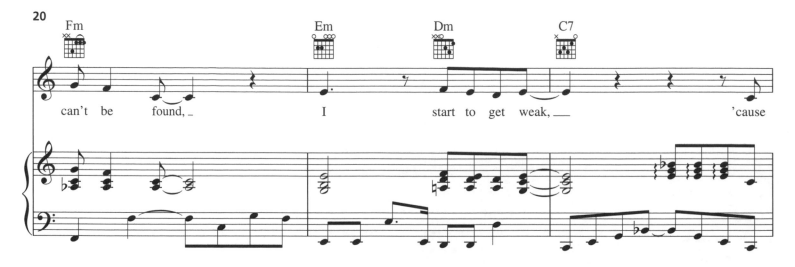

can't be found, __ I start to get weak, ___ 'cause

no one knows __ me un - der - neath these clothes, __ but

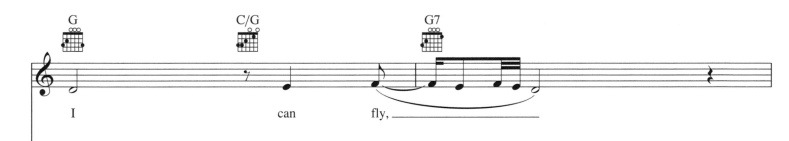

I can fly, _____

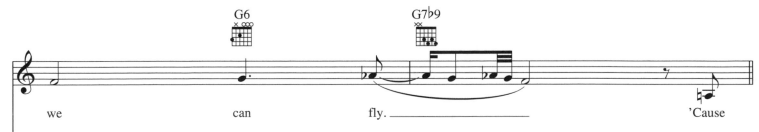

we can fly. _____ 'Cause

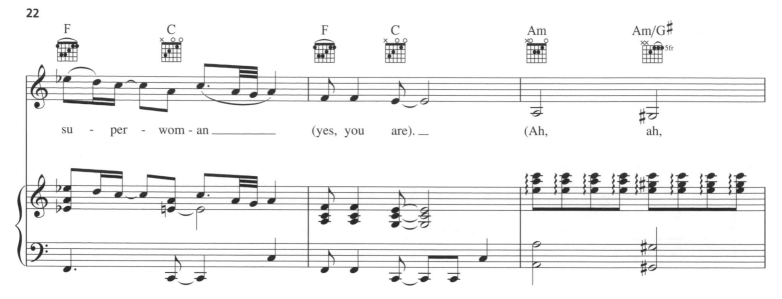

su - per - wom - an _____ (yes, you are). _ (Ah, ah,

ah, ah.) (Nah, nah, nah, nah.)

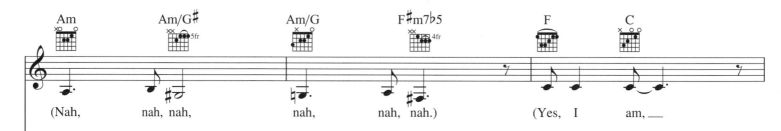

(Nah, nah, nah, nah, nah, nah.) (Yes, I am, _

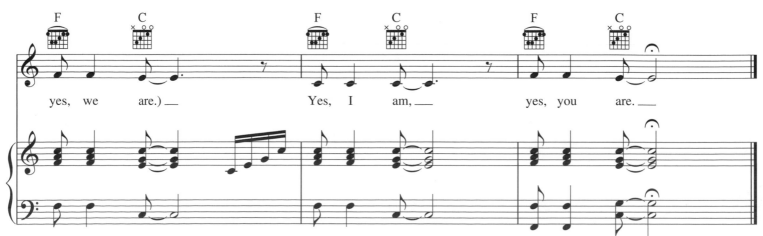

yes, we are.) _ Yes, I am, _ yes, you are. _

NO ONE

Words and Music by ALICIA KEYS,
KERRY BROTHERS, JR. and GEORGE HARRY

Moderately, with a beat

I just want you close _

where you can stay _ for-ev-er. _ You _ can be _

_ sure _ that it will on-ly get bet-ter. _

You__ and me to-geth-er_____ through the days and nights.____

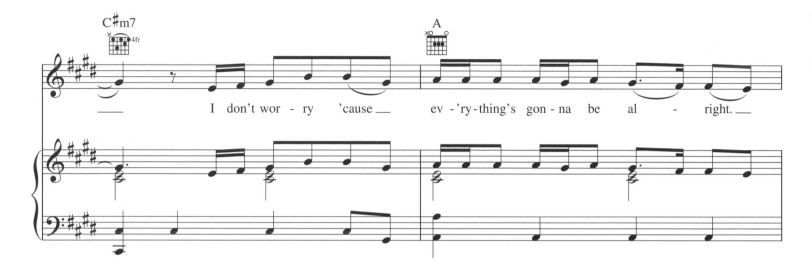

__ I don't wor - ry 'cause __ ev -'ry-thing's gon-na be al - right.__

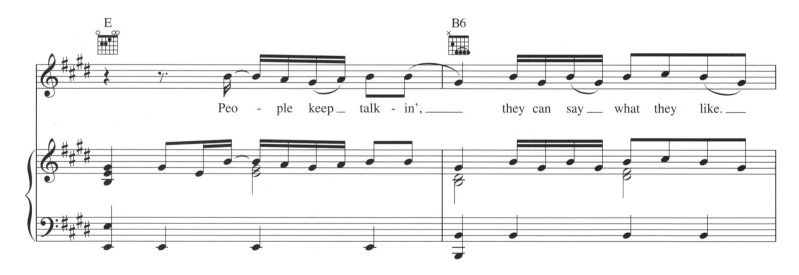

Peo - ple keep__ talk - in',_____ they can say__ what they like.__

But__ all I know__ is ev-'ry-thing's gon-na be al - right.___ And no__ one, no__

one, no one can get in the way of what I'm feel - in'.

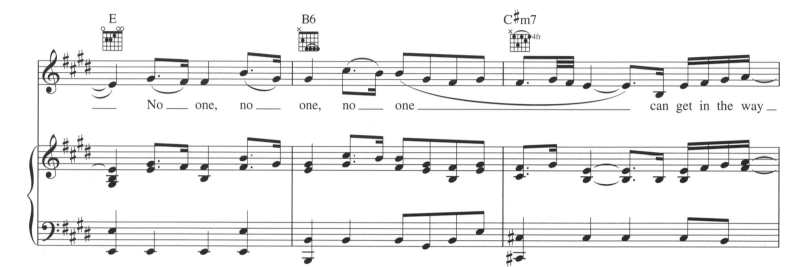

No one, no one, no one can get in the way

of what I feel for you, you, you,

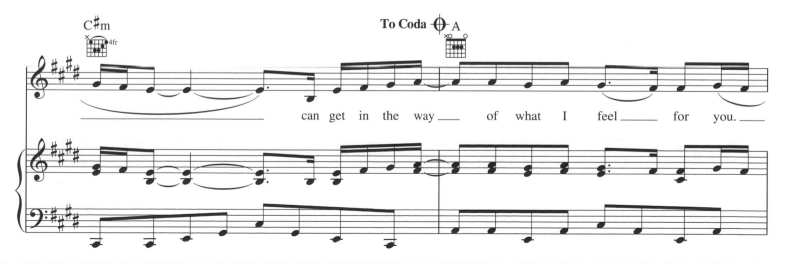

can get in the way of what I feel for you.

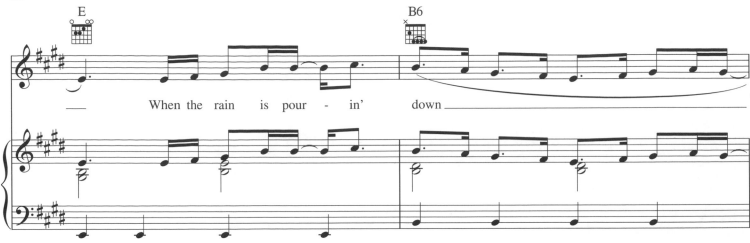

When the rain is pour - in' down

and my heart is hurt - in', you will al - ways be a-

round. This I know for cer - tain.

of what I feel. I know some peo - ple

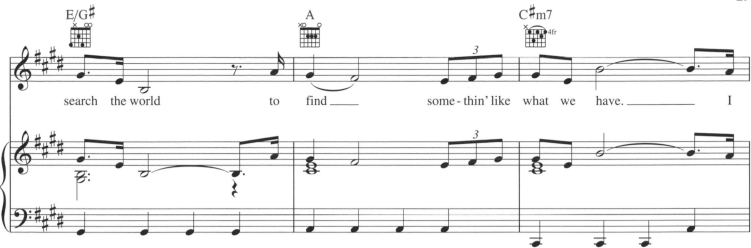

search the world to find _____ some-thin' like what we have. _____ I

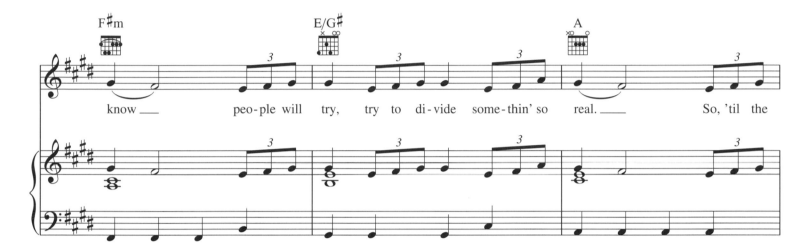

know _____ peo-ple will try, try to di-vide some-thin' so real. _____ So, 'til the

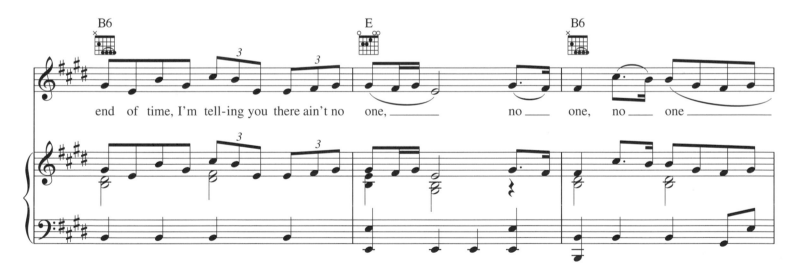

end of time, I'm tell-ing you there ain't no one, _____ no _____ one, no _____ one _____

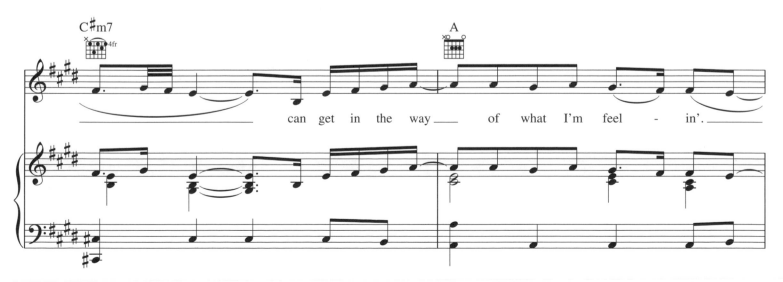

_____ can get in the way _____ of what I'm feel - in'. _____

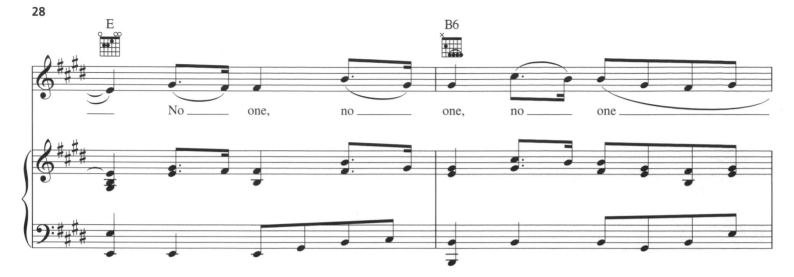

No ___ one, no ___ one, no ___ one

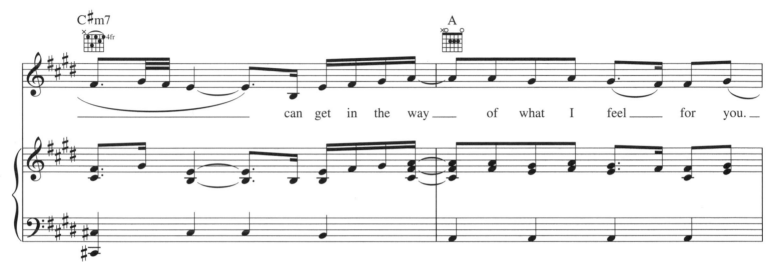

can get in the way ___ of what I feel ___ for you. ___

Oh, oh, oh, oh, oh, oh, oh, oh, oh,

oh, oh, oh, oh, oh, oh, ho, oh, ho, oh, ho, oh, ho, oh. ___ Oh, oh, oh, oh,

oh,   oh, oh, oh, oh,   oh,   oh, oh, oh, oh,   oh, ho, oh, ho, oh, ho, oh, ho,

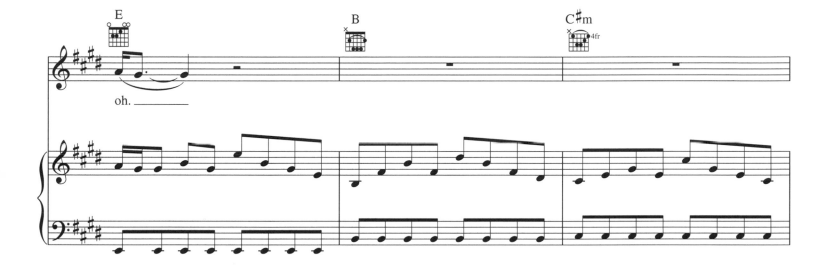

oh. _____

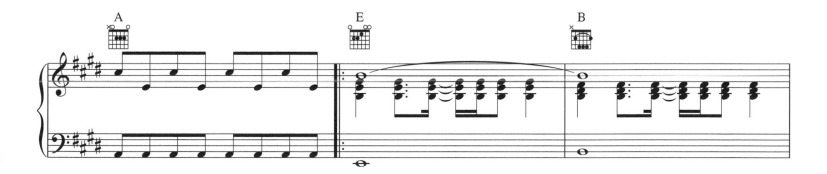

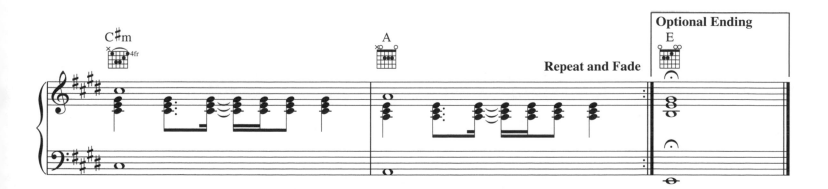

Repeat and Fade

Optional Ending

LIKE YOU'LL NEVER SEE ME AGAIN

Words and Music by ALICIA KEYS
and KERRY BROTHERS, JR.

Relaxed R&B Ballad

If I had no more time, no more time left to be here, _

would you cher - ish what we had? Was it ev - 'ry - thing _ that you were look-ing
Do you know un - til you lose it, that it's ev - 'ry - thing _ that we are look-ing

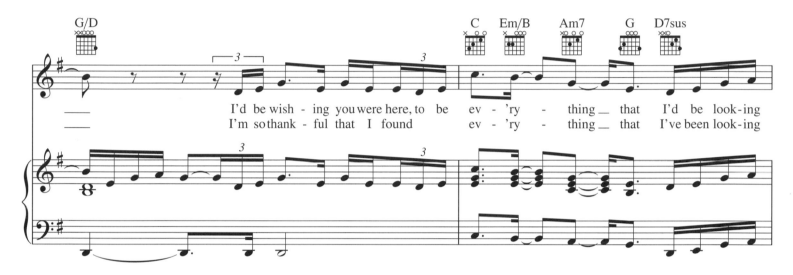

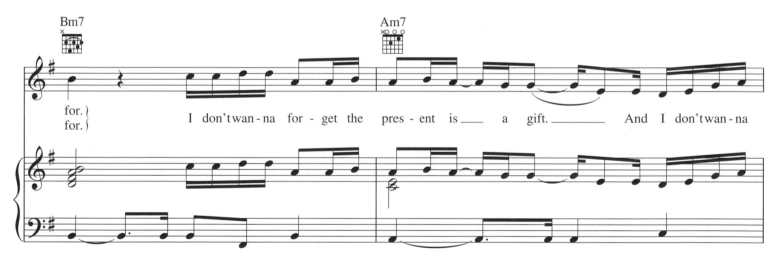

knows an - oth - er day is not real - ly guar - an - teed. _____ So ev - 'ry time you

hold me, hold me like this is the last time. Ev - 'ry time you

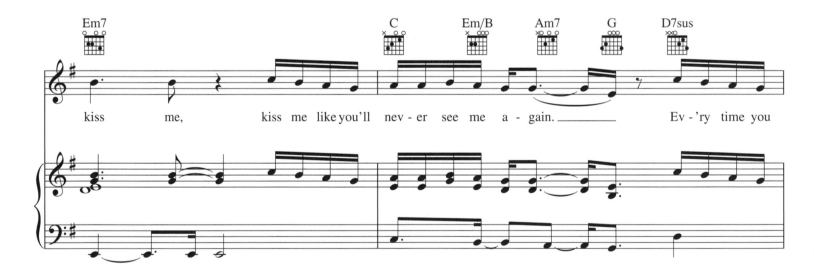

kiss me, kiss me like you'll nev - er see me a - gain. _____ Ev - 'ry time you

touch me, touch me like this is the last time. Prom - ise that you'll

love me, love me like you'll nev-er see me a-gain,_____ oh, oh, oh.__

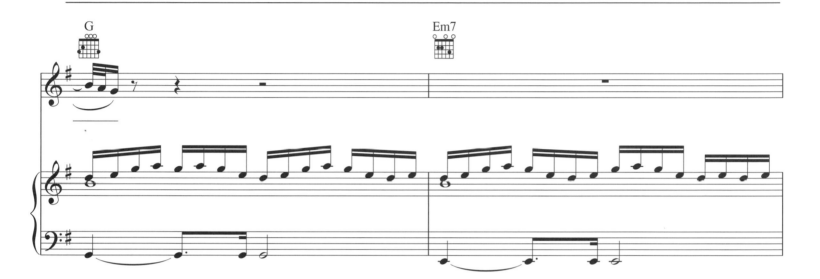

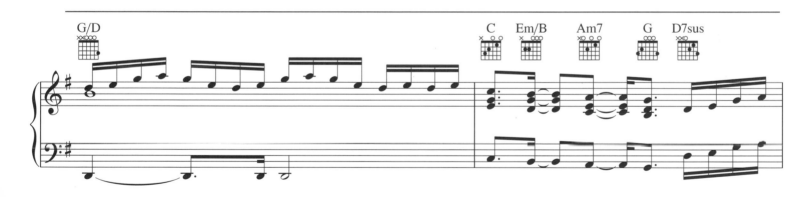

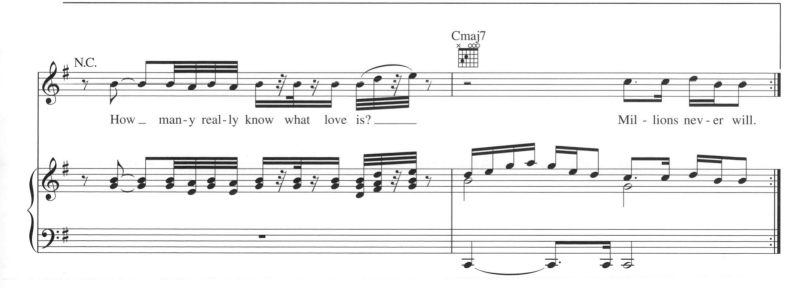

How _ man-y real-ly know what love is? _____ Mil - lions nev-er will.

nev - er see me a - gain. _____ So ev -'ry time you hold me, hold me like this is the

Add lead vocal ad lib.

last time. Ev -'ry time you kiss me, kiss me like you'll

nev - er see me a - gain. _____ Ev -'ry time you touch me, touch me like this is the

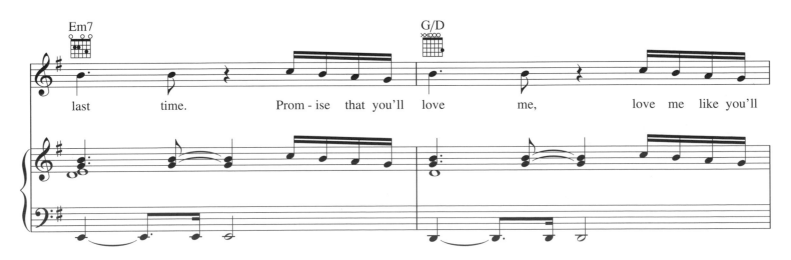

last time. Prom - ise that you'll love me, love me like you'll

nev - er see me a - gain, _____ oh, oh, oh. (Oh, ___ oh, ___ oh.) _____
End vocal ad lib.

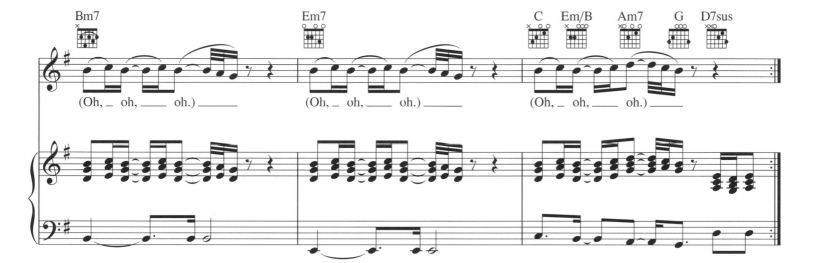

(Oh, _ oh, ___ oh.) _____ (Oh, _ oh, ___ oh.) _____ (Oh, _ oh, ___ oh.) _____

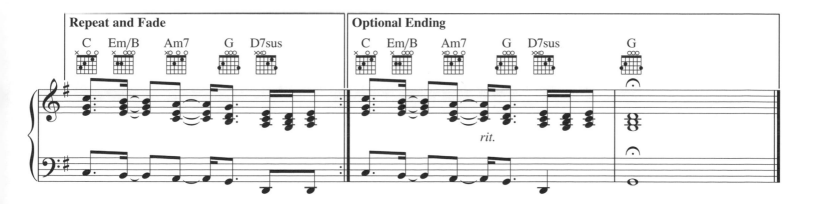

Repeat and Fade

Optional Ending

rit.

LESSON LEARNED

Words and Music by ALICIA KEYS,
RAPHAEL SAADIQ and JOHN MAYER

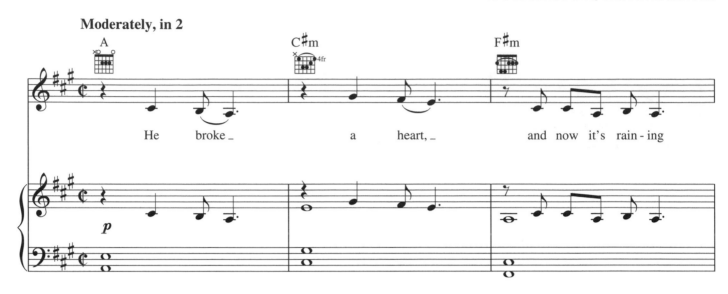

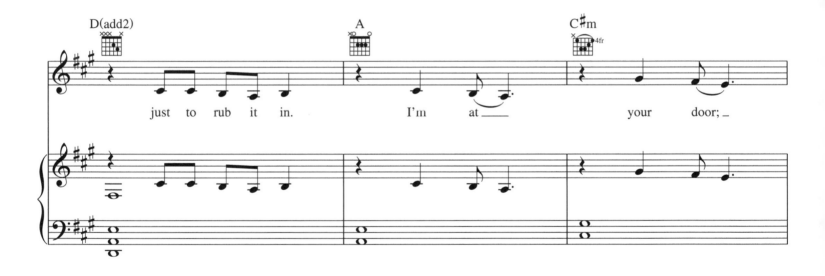

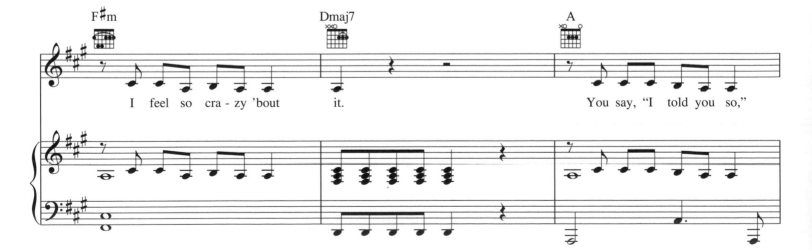

you saw it long a - go, you knew he had to go.

I fin -'lly came a - round; I'm back on sol - id ground, can't let it get me down.

(It's al - right, it's al - right,

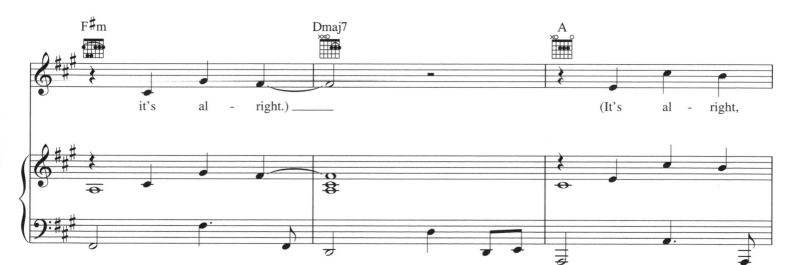

it's al - right.) _____ (It's al - right,

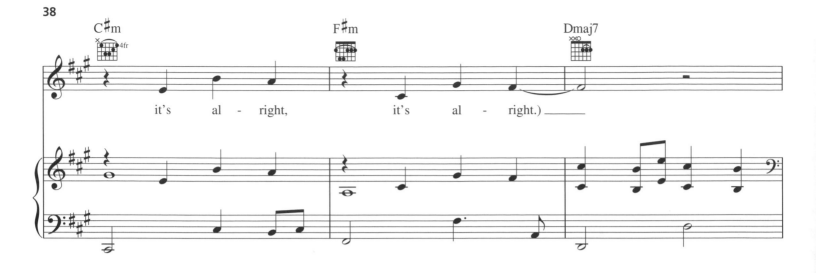

it's al - right, it's al - right.) ____

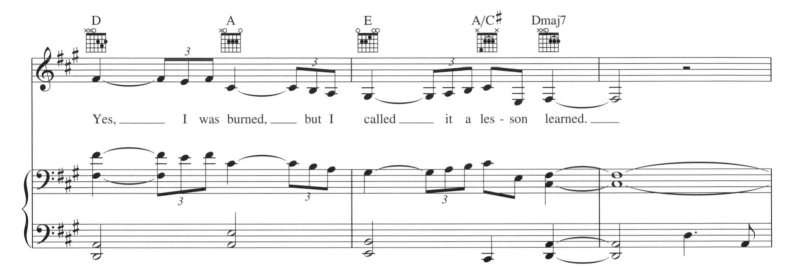

Yes, ____ I was burned, ____ but I called ____ it a les - son learned. ____

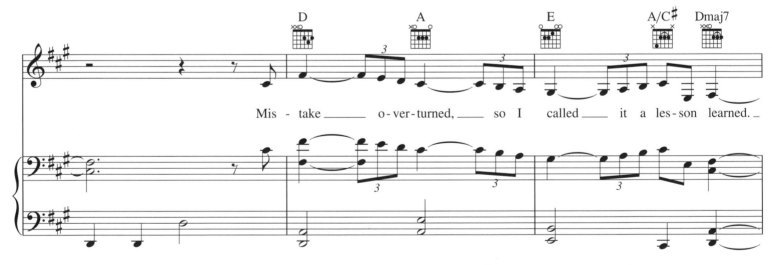

Mis - take ____ o - ver - turned, ____ so I called ____ it a les - son learned. ____

My soul ____ is re - turned, ____ so I

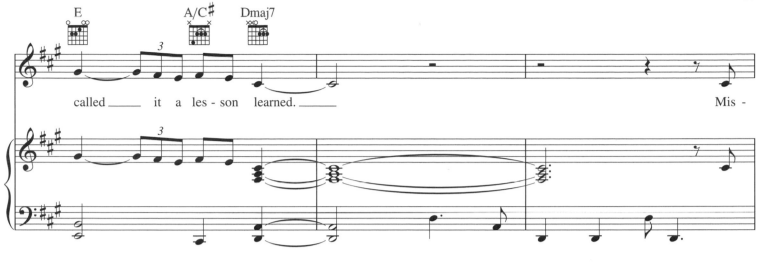

called _____ it a les - son learned. _____ Mis -

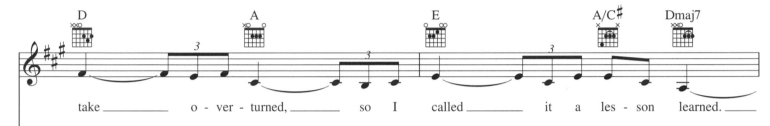

take _____ o - ver - turned, _____ so I called _____ it a les - son learned. _____

My soul _____ has re - turned, _____ so I

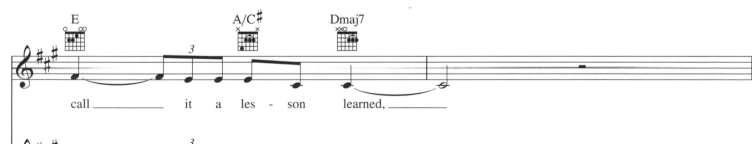

call _____ it a les - son learned, _____

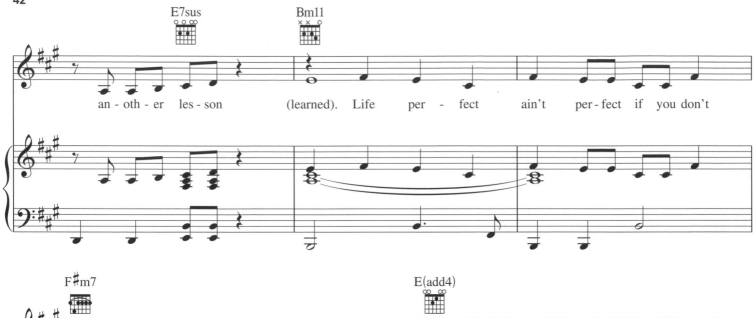

an - oth - er les - son (learned). Life per - fect ain't per - fect if you don't

know what the strug - gle's for. ____

Fall - ing down ain't fall - ing down if you don't cry when you hit the floor. __

It's called the past 'cause I'm get - tin' past and I ain't

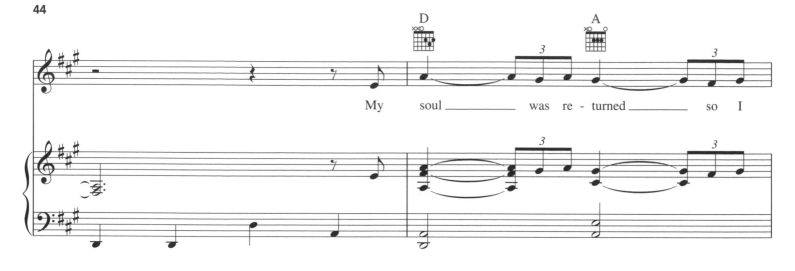

My soul _____ was re-turned _____ so I

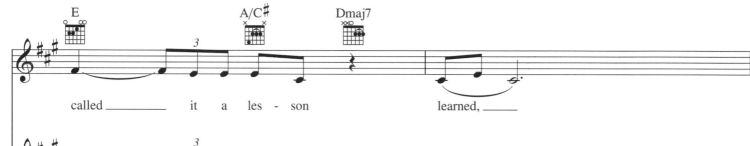

called _____ it a les-son learned, _____

an-oth-er les-son learned. ___ Sing-in',

yes, _____ I was burned, ___ but I called it a les-son learned.

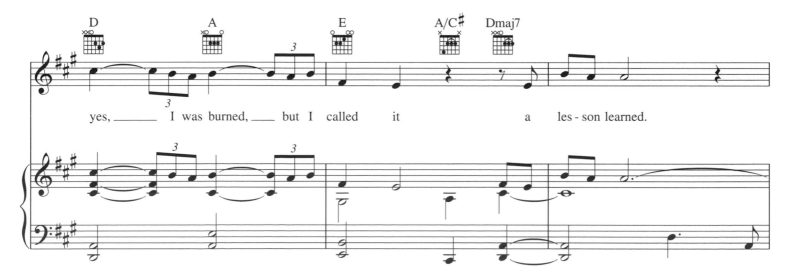

Said mis - take's _____ o - ver - turned, _____ so I

called _____ it a les - son learned. _____ My

soul _____ has re - turned, _____ so I called it _____ les - son learned, ___ oh, ___

les - son learned. ____ (It's al - right, it's a les - son learned.) ___

WRECKLESS LOVE

Words and Music by ALICIA KEYS,
JACK SPLASH and HAROLD LILLY, JR.

* Recorded a half step lower.

did-n't know me, did-n't need me, want to touch me, could-n't leave me,

I could-n't know how far this would go, I could-n't know if this was for sure.

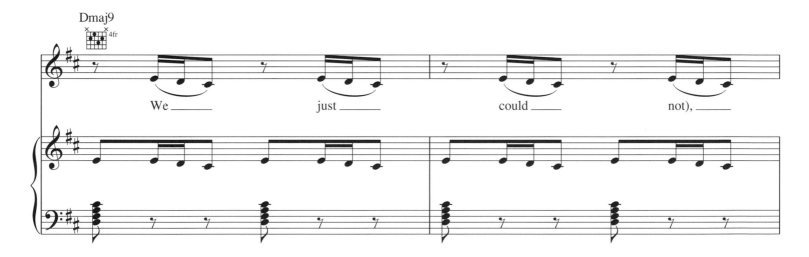

We ___ just ___ could ___ not), ___

we just could not get e-nough of it, ba-by. Let's go ___ have that

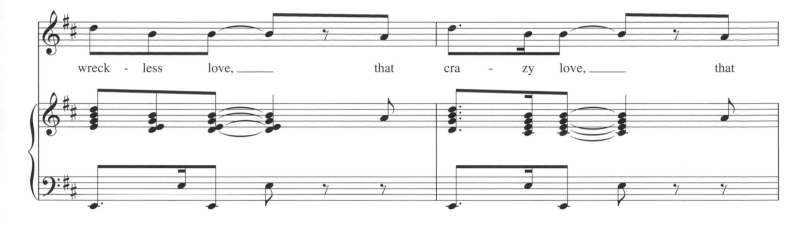

wreck - less love, _____ that cra - zy love, _____ that

off the wall, "won't stop 'til I get e - nough" kind of love.

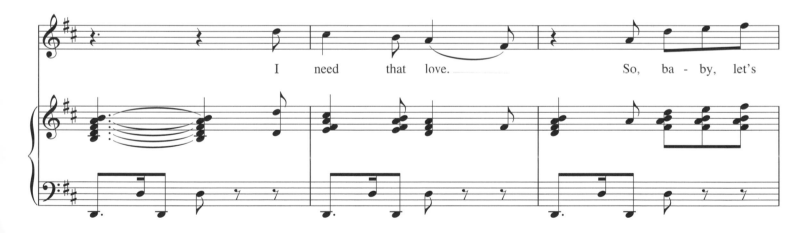

I need that love. _____ So, ba - by, let's

go _____ have that wreck - less love, _____ that

cra - zy love, _____ that "I don't real - ly care, we can have it an - y-

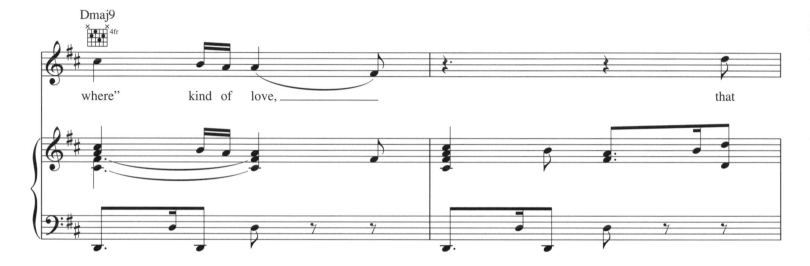

Dmaj9

where" kind of love, _____ that

To Coda

wreck - less love. _____

Em9

Let's go back in time, when our kiss was brand - new,

an ad - ven - ture, not per - fect - ed, 'lit - tle hes - i - tant; let's

Dmaj9

go back there ___ (go back there); ___ let's take it there ___

Em9

Ooh, ba - by, now, ___ take it back in time, when for -
(take it there). ___

ev - er was a min - ute and e - ter - ni - ty was a sec - ond. I'm

D.S. al Coda

CODA

stress - in' that we gon - na   Oh _____ ba - by, let's

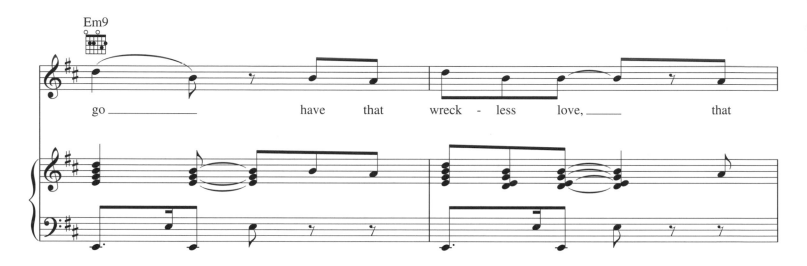

Em9

go _____ have that wreck - less love, _____ that

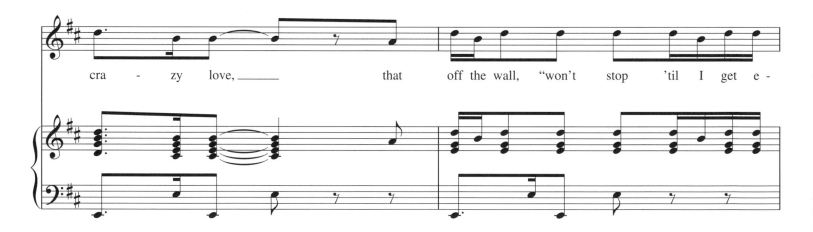

cra - zy love, _____ that off the wall, "won't stop 'til I get e-

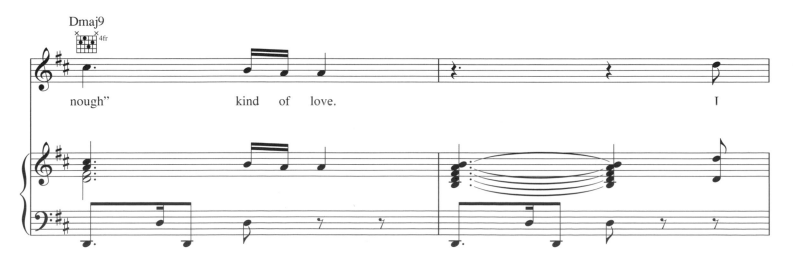

Dmaj9

nough" _____ kind of love.   I

need that love. _____ So, ba - by, let's go _____ have that

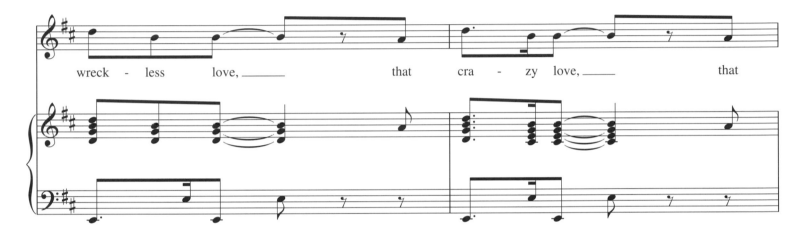

wreck - less love, _____ that cra - zy love, _____ that

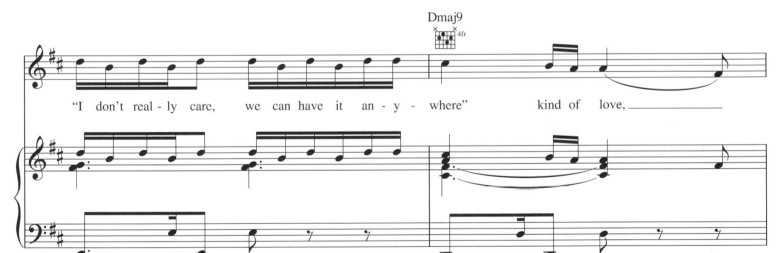

"I don't real - ly care, we can have it an - y - where" kind of love, _____

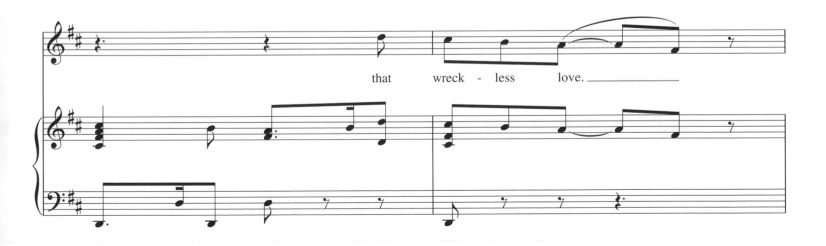

that wreck - less love. _____

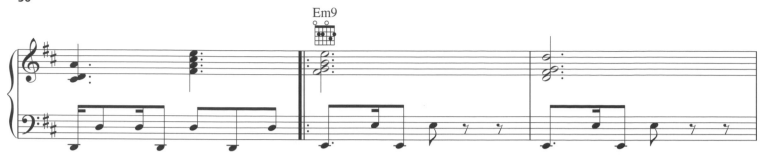

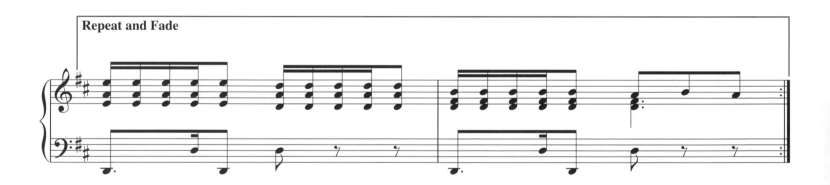

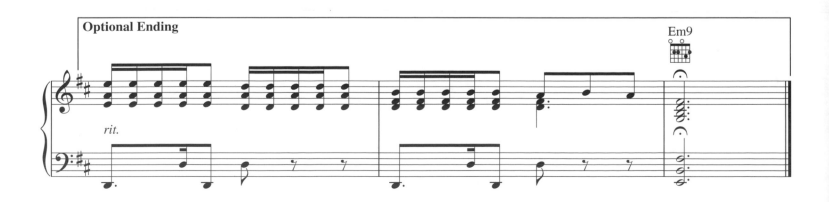

THE THING ABOUT LOVE

Words and Music by ALICIA KEYS
and LINDA PERRY

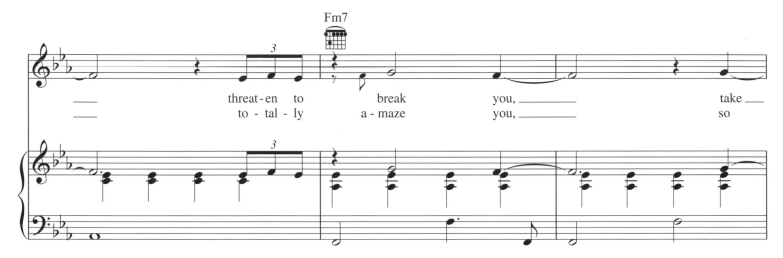

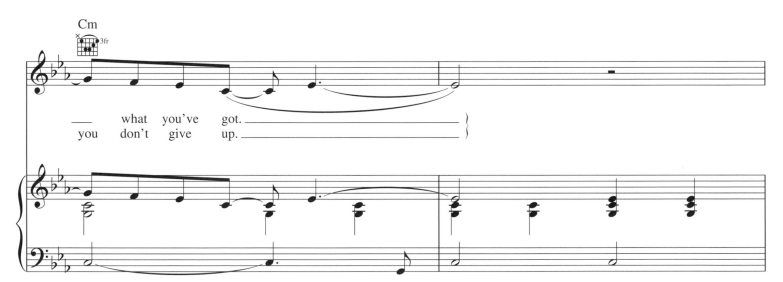

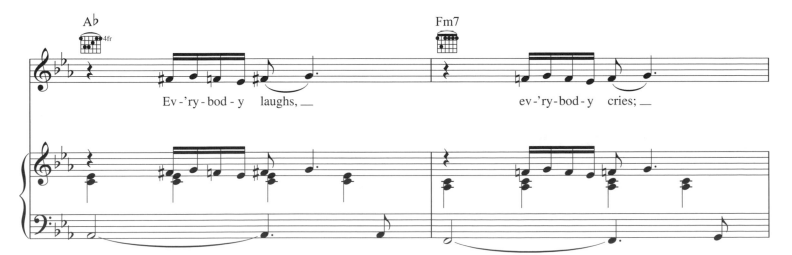

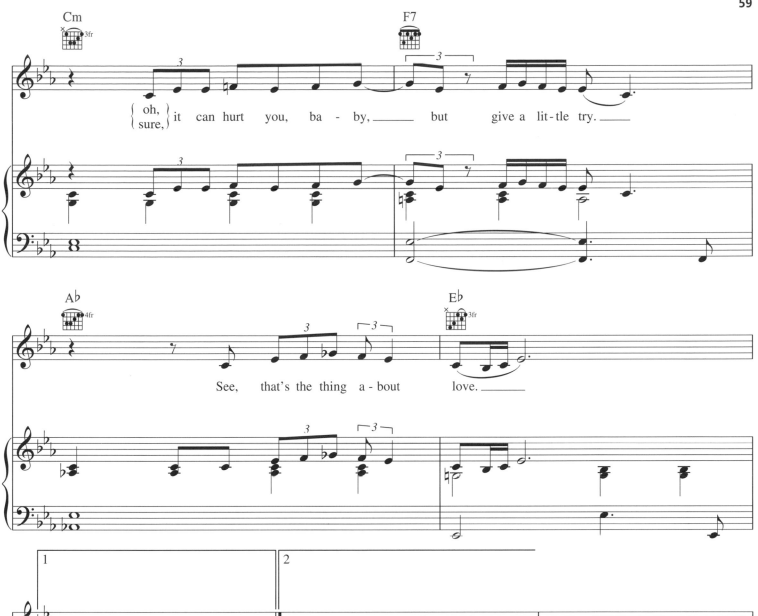

oh,
sure, } it can hurt you, ba - by, ____ but give a lit-tle try. ____

See, that's the thing a - bout love. ____

Oh,

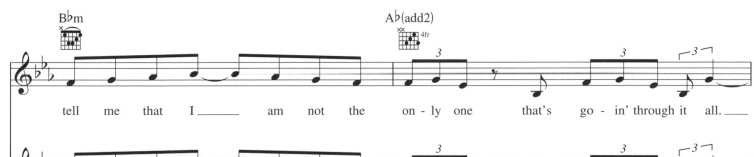

tell me that I ____ am not the on - ly one that's go - in' through it all. ____

it's 'bout time _____ for me to

Slower, expressively

shine. _____

'Cause ev-'ry-bod-y laughs _____ and ev-'ry-bod-y cries. _____

Sure, it could hurt you, ba - by, but give it a lit-tle try. _____

TEENAGE LOVE AFFAIR

Words and Music by ALICIA KEYS, JACK SPLASH,
HAROLD LILLY, JR., CARL HAMPTON,
JO BRIDGES and and TOM NIXON

Recorded a half step lower.

I just don't want to say good-bye, 'cause you are my ba-by, ba-by.

Noth - in' real - ly mat - ters;

I don't real-ly care what no-bod-y tell ____

____ me; I'm gon-na be here. It's a

mat - ter of ex - treme im - por - tance, my first teen - age love

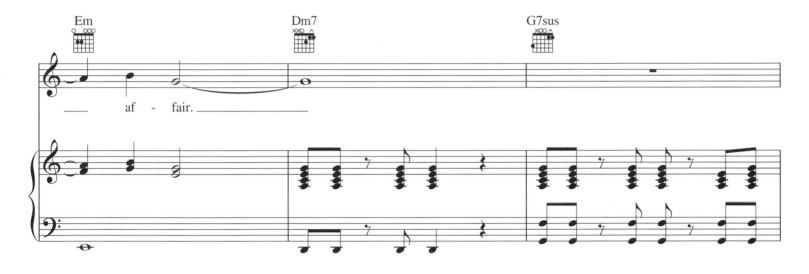

af - fair.

(Spoken:) Hey, boy... *so,*

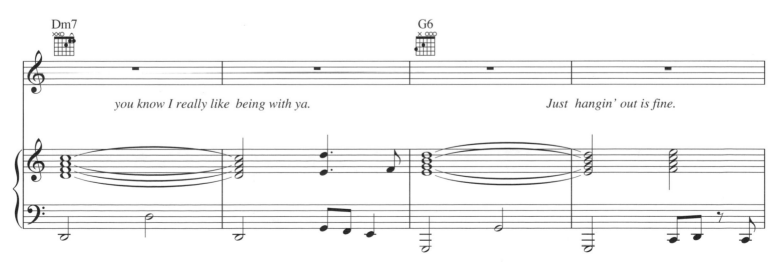

you know I really like being with ya. *Just hangin' out is fine.*

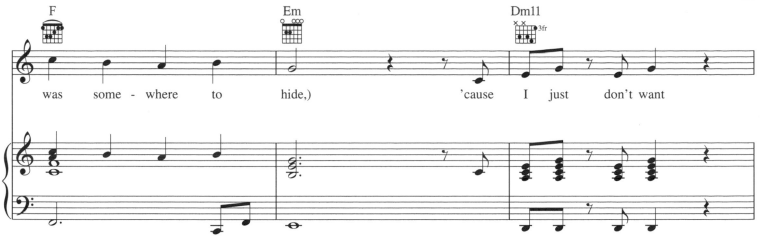

was some-where to hide,) 'cause I just don't want

to say good-bye, 'cause you are my ba-by, ba-by. Noth-in'

real-ly mat-ters; I don't real-ly care what no-

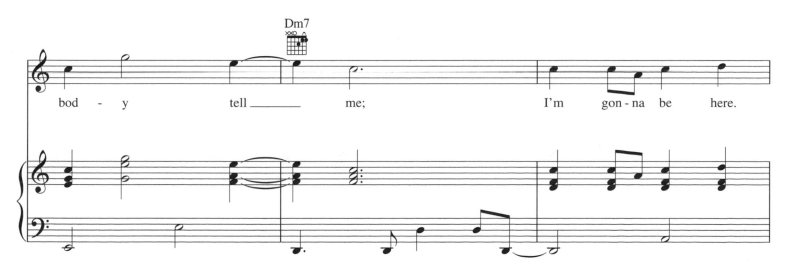

bod-y tell _____ me; I'm gon-na be here.

I NEED YOU

Words and Music by ALICIA KEYS, PAUL GREEN,
HAROLD LILLY, JR. and MARK BATSON

the sky can't wait

for the light of the sun.

So how could you

look me in my eye and not see what,

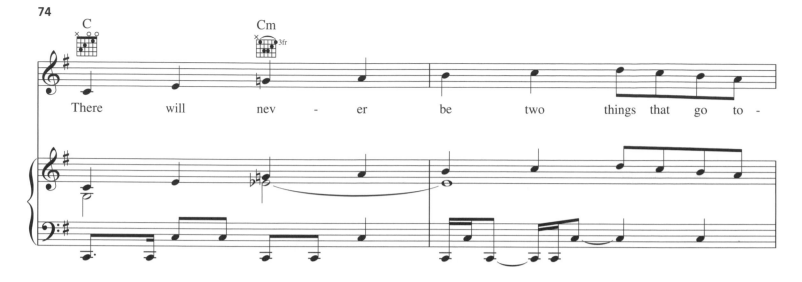

There will nev - er be two things that go to -

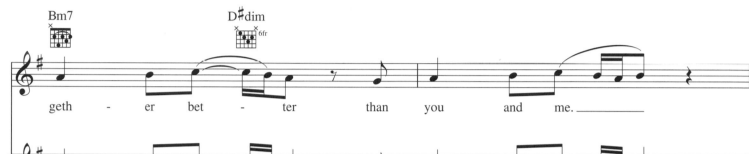

geth - er bet - ter than you and me. _____

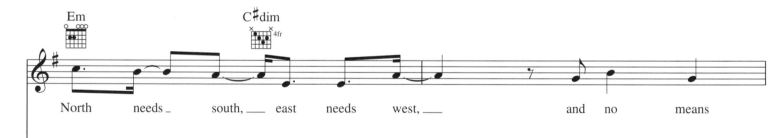

North needs ___ south, ___ east needs west, ___ and no means

yes, yes, yes. _____

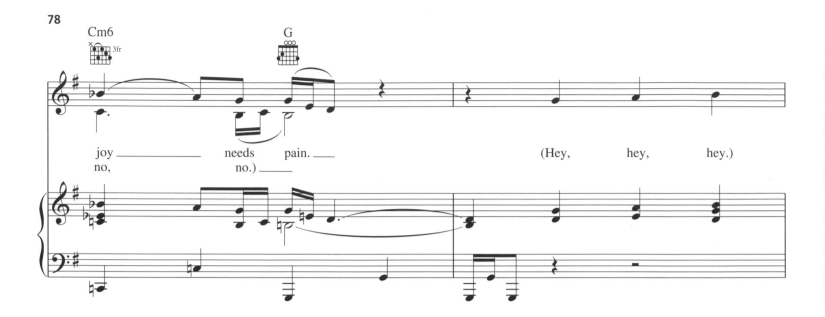

joy _____ needs pain. _____ (Hey, hey, hey.)
no, no.) _____

(Hey, hey, hey.)

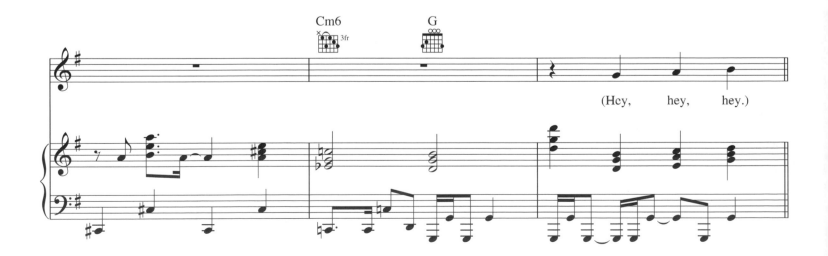

(Hey, hey, hey.)

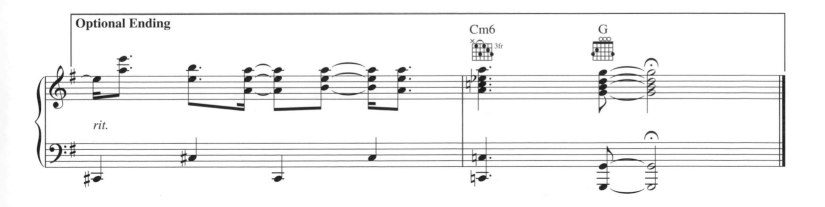

WHERE DO WE GO FROM HERE

Words and Music by ALICIA KEYS,
KERRY BROTHERS, JR., HAROLD LILLY, JR.,
JOSEPH FRIERSON and MARY FRIERSON

Moderately

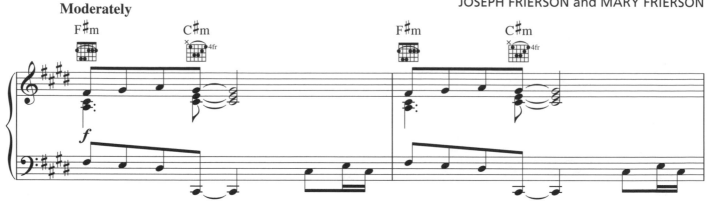

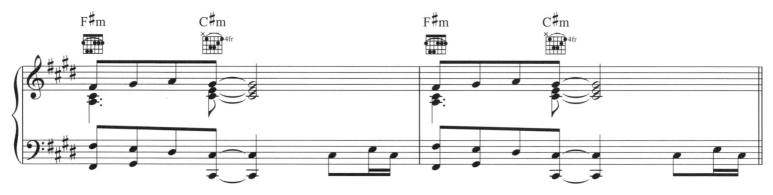

We're at the cross - roads, _ my dear. _

Where do _ we go _ from

here? _____ May-be you won't

go; _____ may-be you'll stay. _____ Oh, _____ I know _____

_____ I'm ___ gon-na miss you ___ ei - ther way. ___

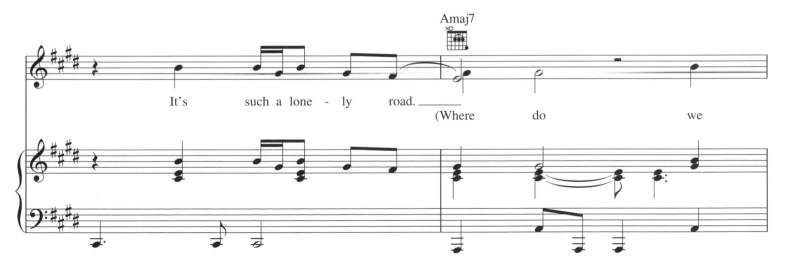

It's such a lone - ly road. _____
(Where do we

go _____ from here?) All I can do is

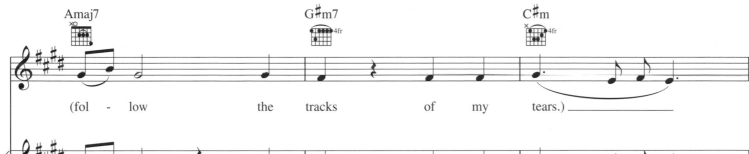

(fol - low the tracks of my tears.) _____

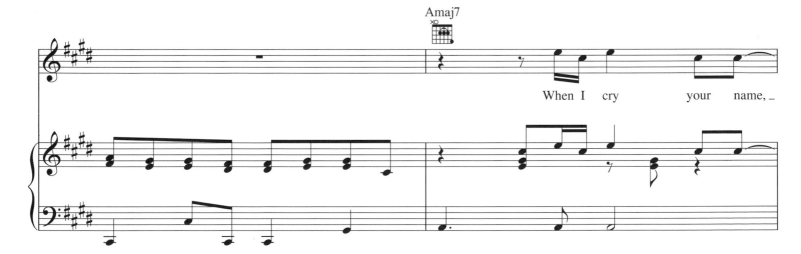

When I cry your name, _

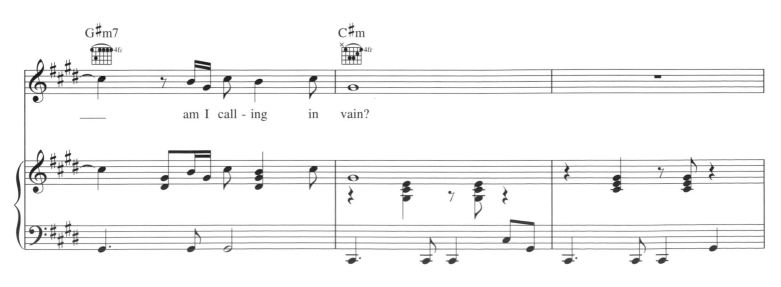

_____ am I call - ing in vain?

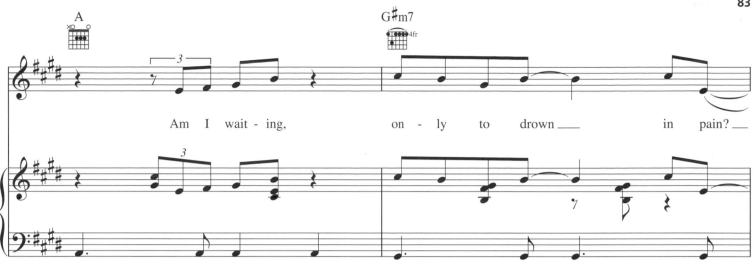

Am I wait - ing, on - ly to drown ___ in pain? ___

___ Don't you do it, don't, ___

___ said don't you leave me this way. ___

I don't know ___ if I can

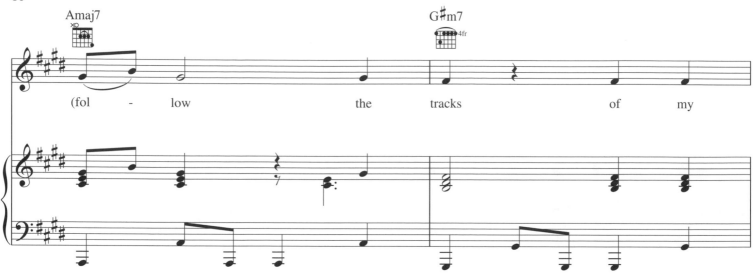

(fol - low   the   tracks   of   my

tears.) _____

tears.) _____

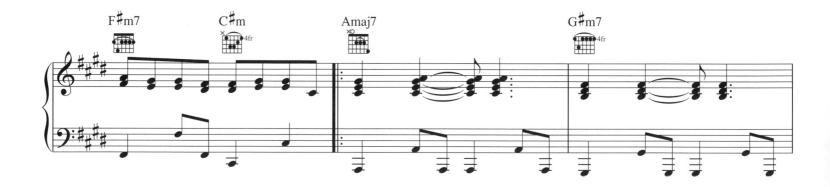

Repeat and Fade

Optional Ending

rit.

PRELUDE TO A KISS

Words and Music by
ALICIA KEYS

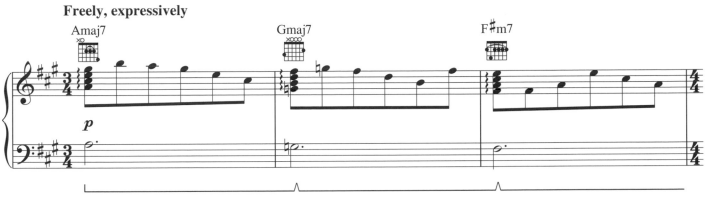

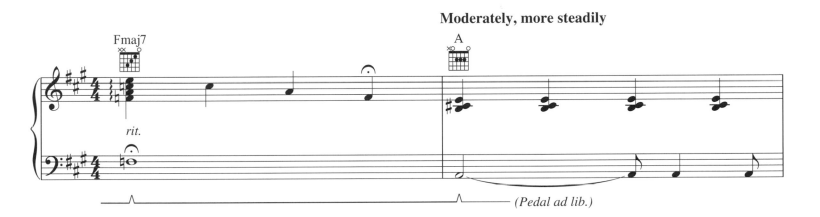

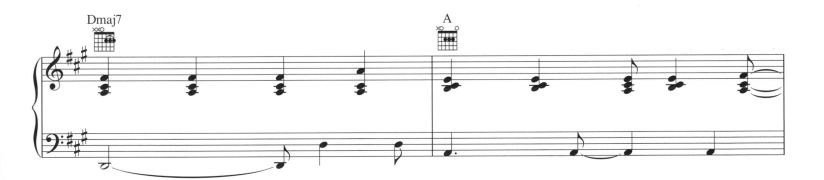

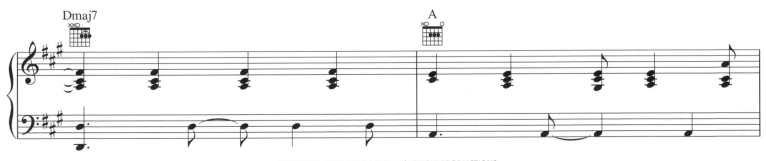

Some-times

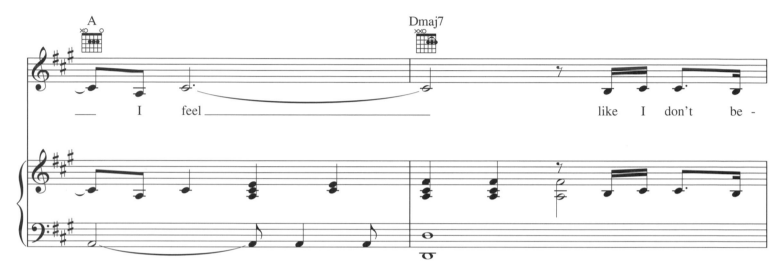

I feel like I don't be-

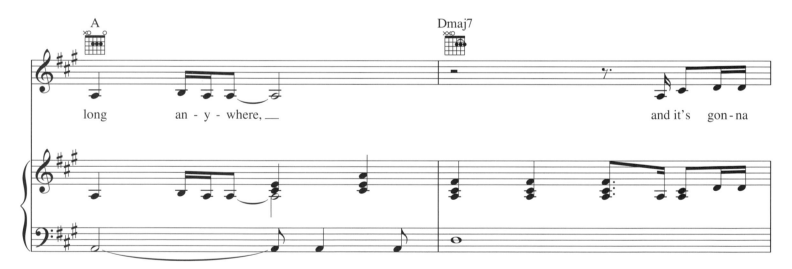

long an-y-where, and it's gon-na

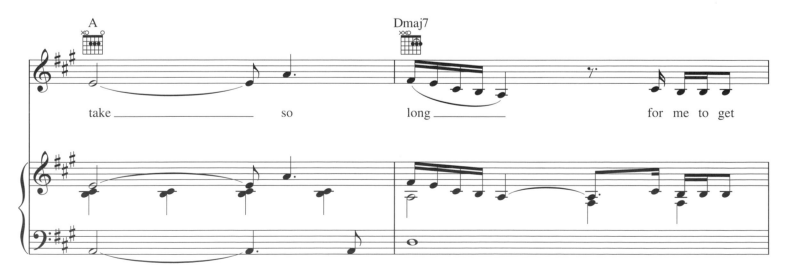

take so long for me to get

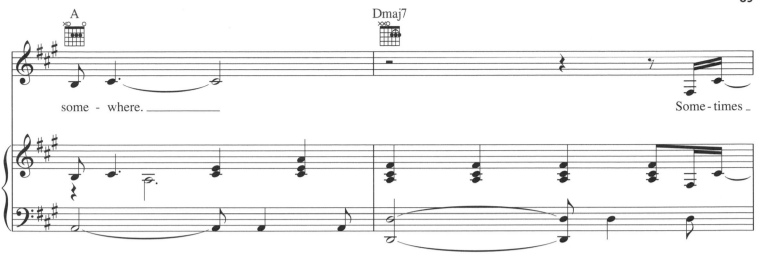

some - where. _____ Some - times _

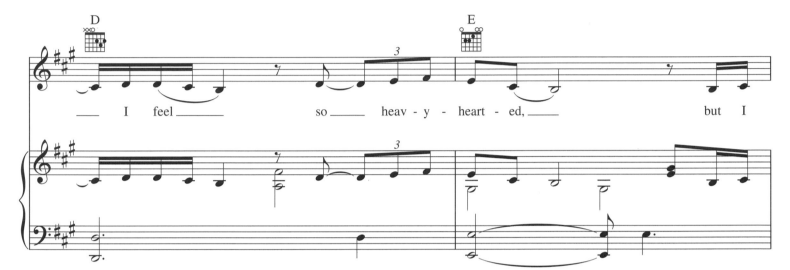

_____ I feel _____ so _____ heav - y - heart - ed, _____ but I

can't ex - plain, 'cause I'm _ so guard - ed. _____ But that's a

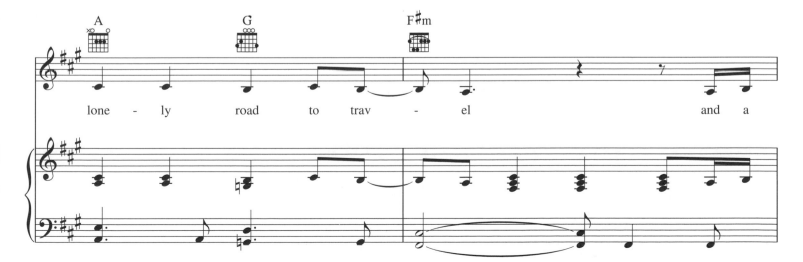

lone - ly road to trav - el _____ and a

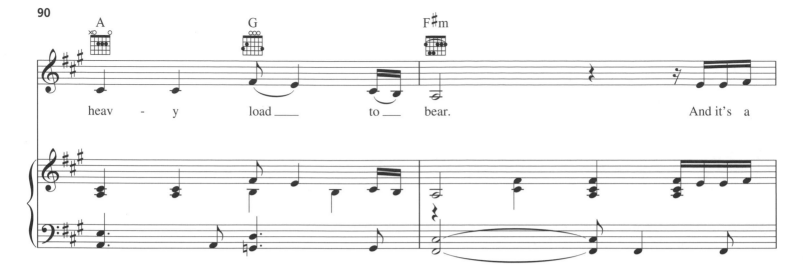

heav - y load ___ to ___ bear. And it's a

long, long _ way ___ to heav - en, _____ but I got - ta

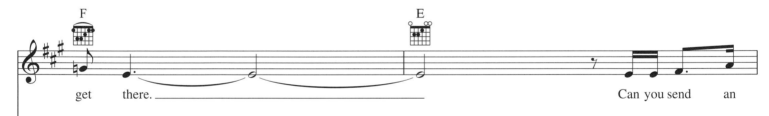

get there. _____ Can you send an

an - gel? Can you send me an

an - gel _____ to guide _____

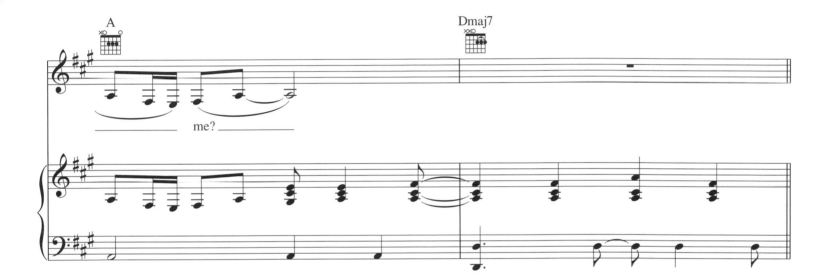

_____ me? _____

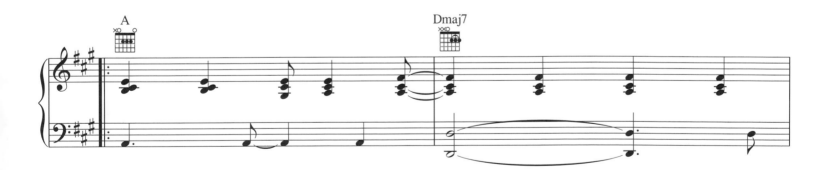

Repeat ad lib. and Fade

Optional Ending

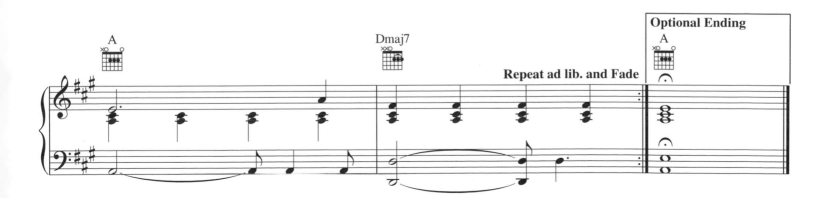

TELL YOU SOMETHING
(Nana's Reprise)

Words and Music by ALICIA KEYS, KERRY BROTHERS, JR.,
ALONZO STEVENSON, PAUL GREEN,
RAY HANEY and STEVE MOSTYN

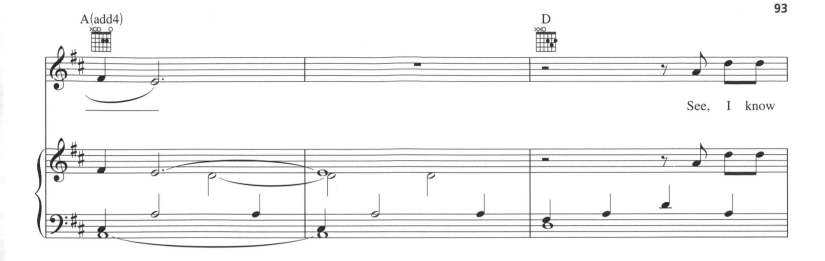

See, I know

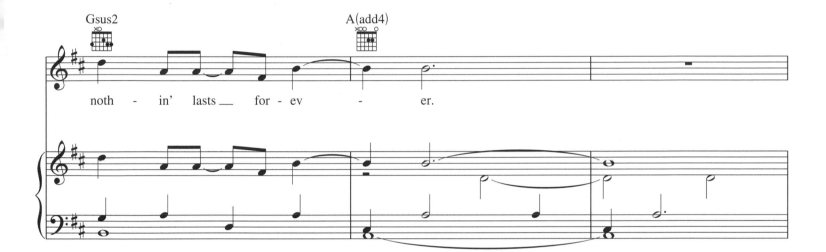

noth - in' lasts __ for - ev - er.

I - mag - ine there was no to - mor - row, _____ I - mag - ine

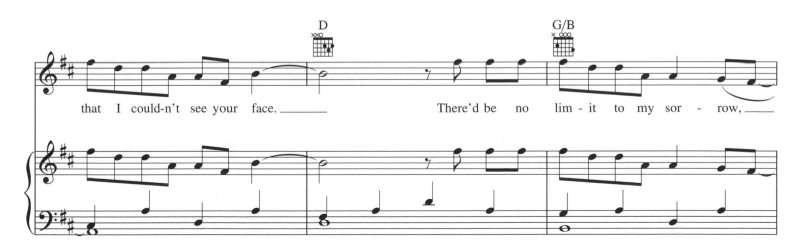

that I could-n't see your face. _____ There'd be no lim - it to my sor - row, ___

waste an-oth-er hour, __ let a-lone an-oth-er day. _____ I wan-na

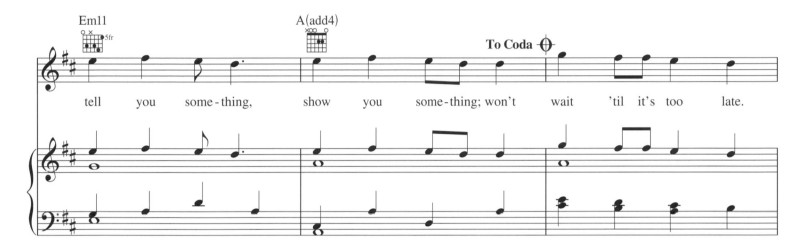

tell you some-thing, show you some-thing; won't wait 'til it's too late.

I can't wait, __ I can't wait, ___ I won't wait, __ I don't wan-na wait.

I can't wait, __ I can't wait, ___ I won't wait, __ I don't wan-

na wait. Won't wait 'til it's too late. _____ Just a

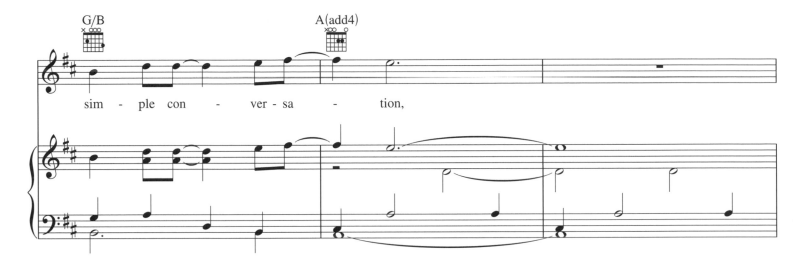

sim - ple con - ver - sa - tion,

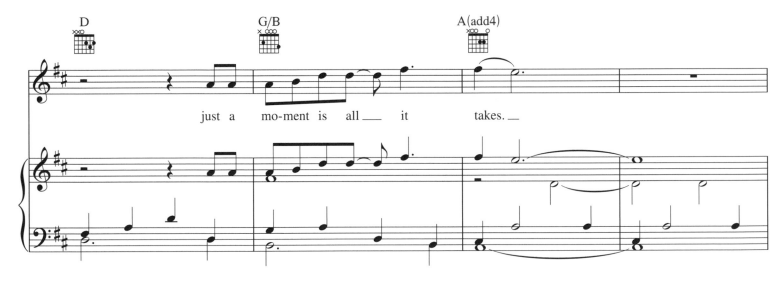

just a mo-ment is all ___ it takes. _

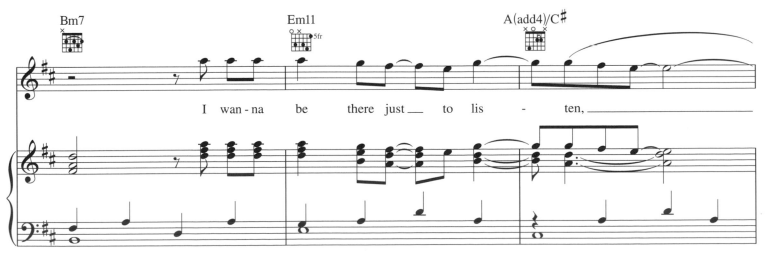

I wan - na be there just ___ to lis - ten, _____

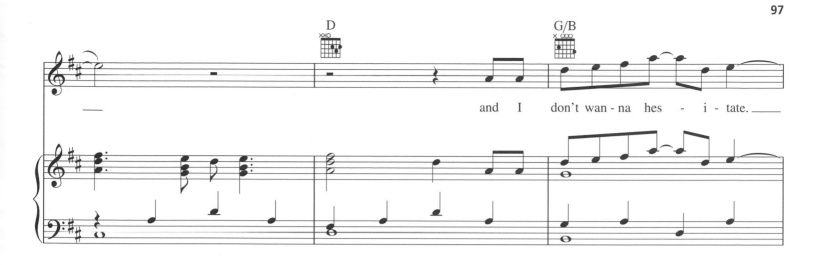

and I don't wan-na hes - i - tate. ___

I - mag - ine

there was no to - mor - row, _____ i - mag - ine that I could-n't see your face. __

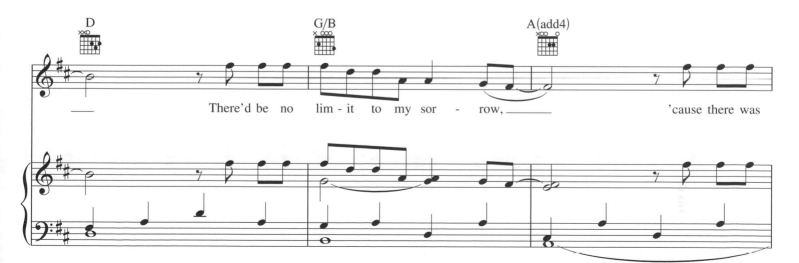

There'd be no lim - it to my sor - row, _____ 'cause there was

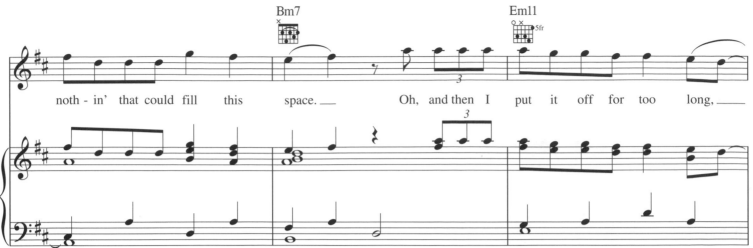

noth - in' that could fill this space. ___ Oh, and then I put it off for too long, ___

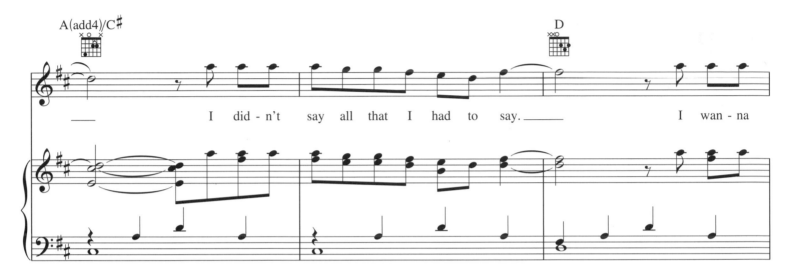

___ I did - n't say all that I had to say. ___ I wan - na

take the time to right the wrong ___ be - fore we get to that place. ___

D.S. al Coda

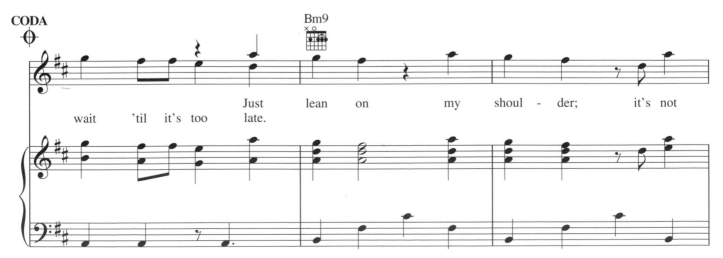

CODA

wait 'til it's too late. Just lean on my shoul - der; it's not

o-ver 'til it's o-ver. Don't wor-ry 'bout it, 'cause I'm

gon-na make sure I'm gon-na get strong-er, yeah.

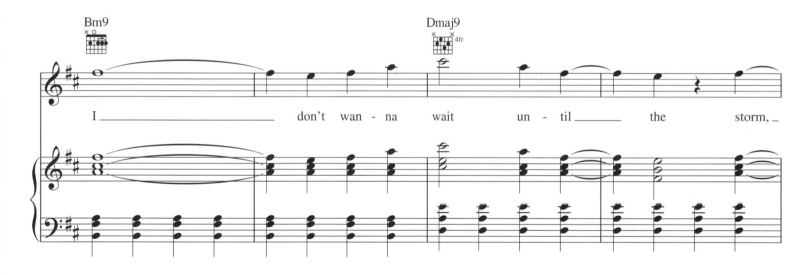

I _____ don't wan-na wait un-til _____ the storm,

when some-thing's wrong _____ and now you're gone _____ and I can't

find ya. I wan-na tell you some-thing,

give you some-thing, show you in so man-y ways, 'cause it would

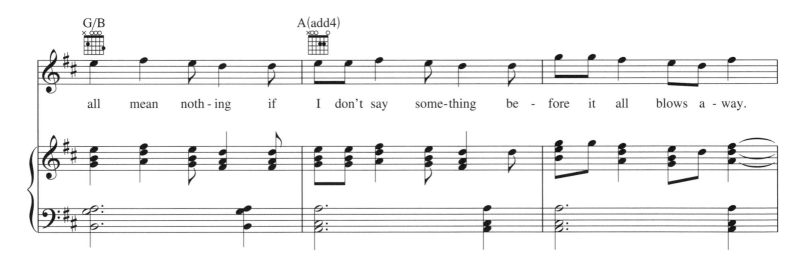

all mean noth-ing if I don't say some-thing be - fore it all blows a - way.

Don't wan - na wait to bring you flow - ers, ___ waste an - oth - er hour, ___

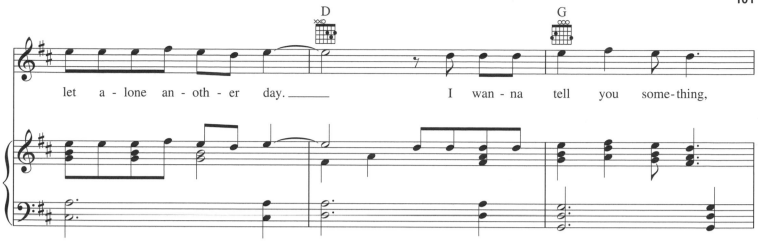

let a-lone an-oth-er day. ____ I wan-na tell you some-thing,

show you some-thing; won't wait 'til it's too late. I can't wait, __ I can't wait, __

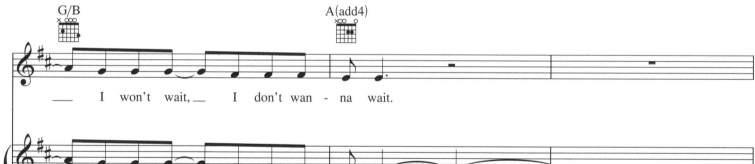

____ I won't wait, __ I don't wan-na wait.

I can't wait, __ I can't wait, ____ I won't wait, __ I don't wan-na wait.

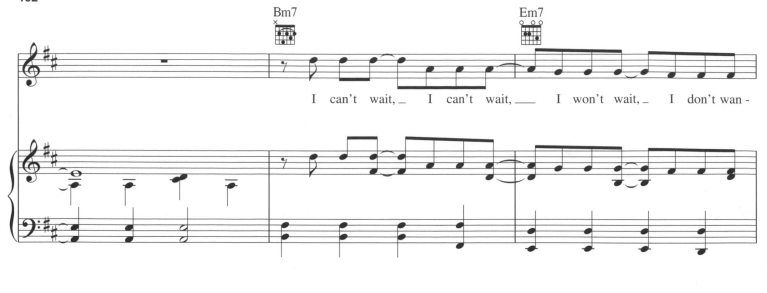

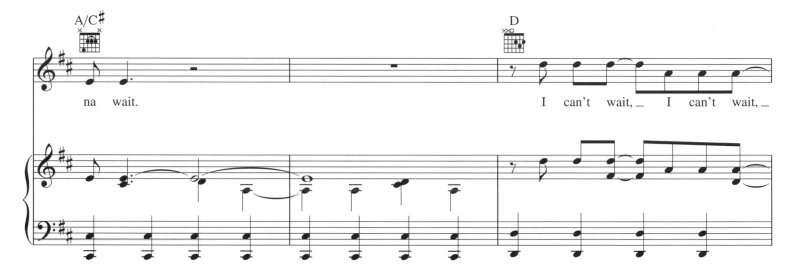

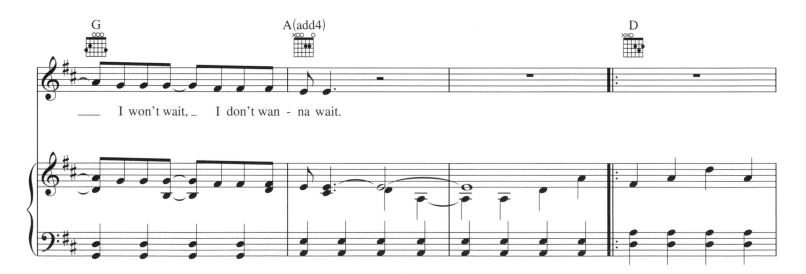

SURE LOOKS GOOD TO ME

Words and Music by ALICIA KEYS
and LINDA PERRY

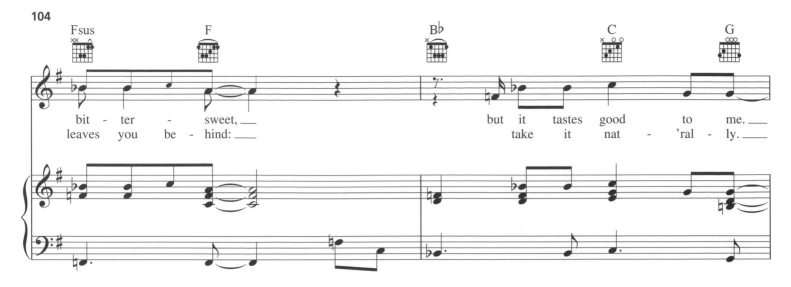

bit - ter - sweet, __ but it tastes good to me. __
leaves you be - hind: __ take it nat - 'ral - ly. __

Take my turn, __ there's
Heav - en knows __ there's

crash and burn: __ that's how it's s'posed to be. __
so much more, __ more than what we see. __

__ So don't rain __ on my pa - rade. __

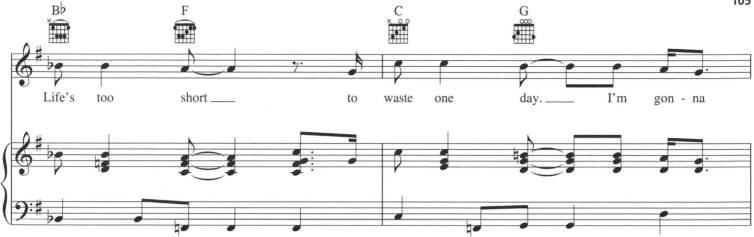

Life's too short ____ to waste one day. ____ I'm gon-na

risk it all, ____ the free-dom to fall. ____ Yes, it

1

sure looks good to me. ____

2

Sure looks good to me. ____

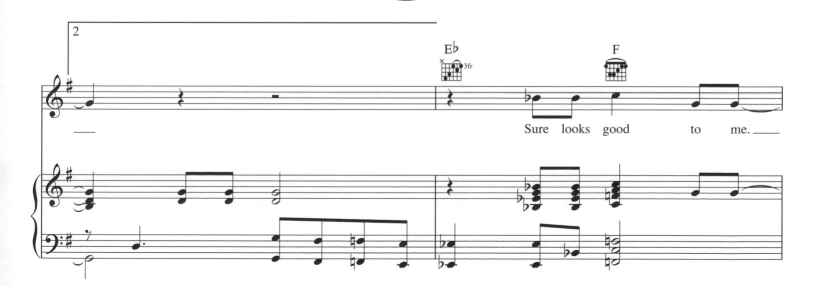

(Hoo,   hoo, _____   ooh, _____   hoo.) _____

Yeah,   yeah,   yeah. _____

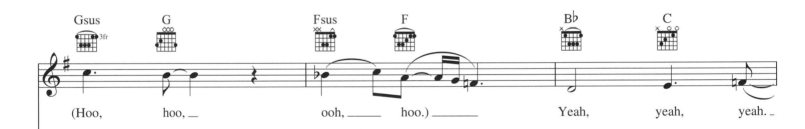

(Hoo,   hoo, _   ooh, _____   hoo.) _____   Yeah,   yeah,   yeah. _

_____   Deep   in my mind _ I'm se - cure, _

we're get-tin' by. ___ Wan-na see the light ___ 'fore I die, ___ 'fore I lie ___

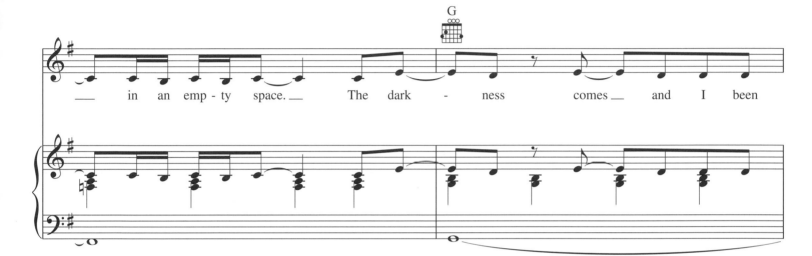

in an emp-ty space. ___ The dark-ness comes ___ and I been

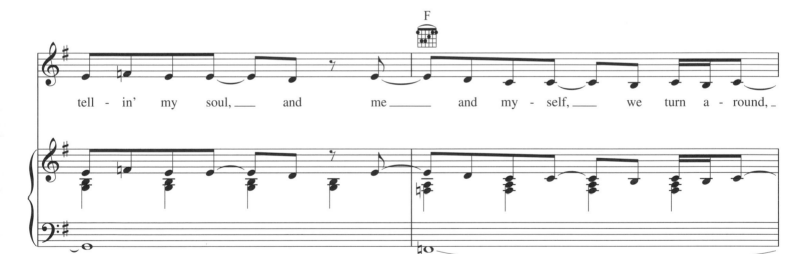

tell-in' my soul, ___ and me ___ and my-self, ___ we turn a-round, ___

we're get-tin' old. ___ But the light-ning crash-in', fool-

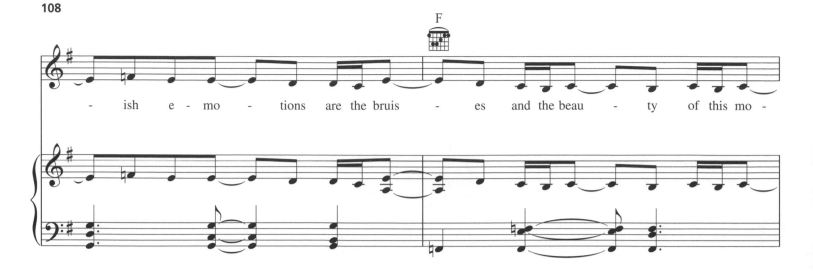

-ish e-mo-tions are the bruis - es and the beau - ty of this mo-

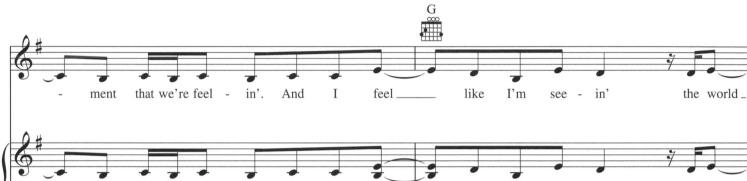

-ment that we're feel - in'. And I feel____ like I'm see - in' the world____

____ in - side of me,____ but I can tell you that I know it's get - tin'

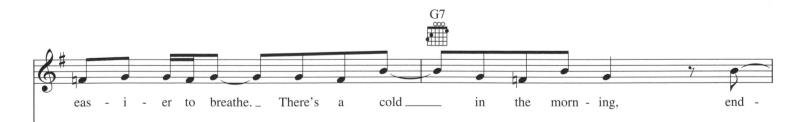

eas - i - er to breathe.____ There's a cold____ in the morn - ing, end-

-less e - qua - tion of who ___ we've be - come. It's a

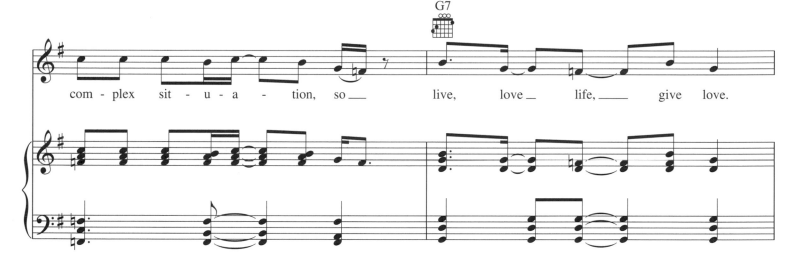

com - plex sit - u - a - tion, so ___ live, love ___ life, ___ give love.

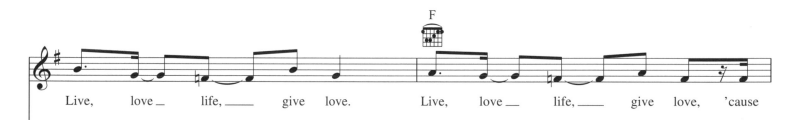

Live, love ___ life, ___ give love. Live, love ___ life, ___ give love, 'cause

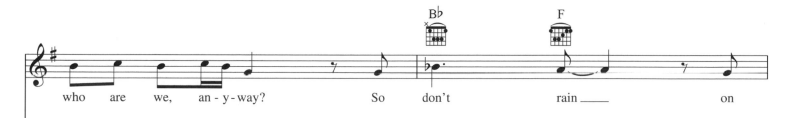

who are we, an - y - way? So don't rain ___ on

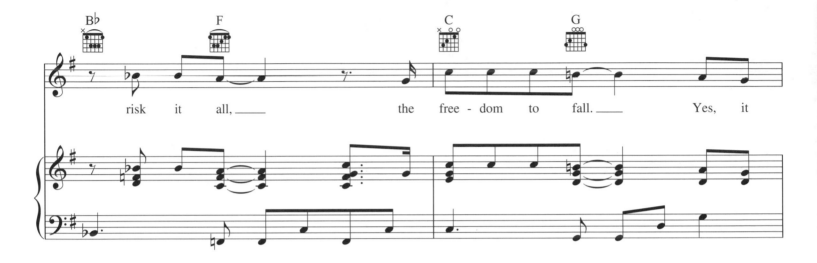

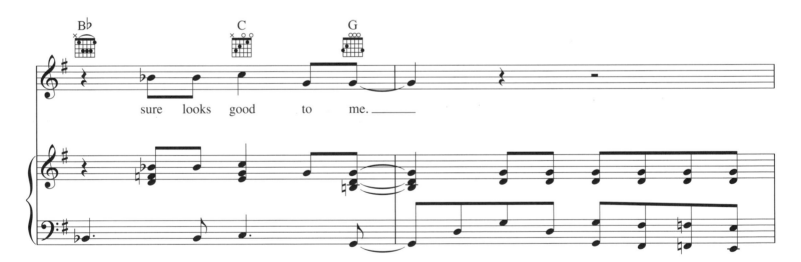